IMAGES OF ENGLAND

WYKE AND LOW MOOR

GREETINGS FROM WYKE

With GREETINGS LOW MOOR. from

IMAGES OF ENGLAND

WYKE AND LOW MOOR

MAUREEN E. BARSTOW, PETER WALKER,
MARY & GEOFF TWENTYMAN

TEMPUS

Frontispiece:
Above: Clockwise from top left: Sparrow Park, Green Lane, St Mary's church, tram terminus, recreation ground.

Below: Clockwise from top left: Wesley Place church and Sunday School, Wesley Place old church and Sunday School, St Mark's church, Holy Trinity church (Wibsey chapel). Centre: chapel at North Bierley cemetery.

First published 2005

Tempus Publishing Limited
The Mill, Brimscombe Port,
Stroud, Gloucestershire, GL5 2QG
www.tempus-publishing.com

© Maureen E. Barstow, Peter Walker,
Mary Twentyman and Geoff Twentyman, 2005

The right of Maureen E. Barstow, Peter Walker, Mary Twentyman and Geoff Twentyman to be identified as the Author of this work has been asserted in accordance with the Copyrights, Designs and Patents Act 1988.

British Library Cataloguing in Publication Data.
A catalogue record for this book is available from the British Library.

ISBN 0 7524 3514 0

Typesetting and origination by Tempus Publishing Limited.
Printed in Great Britain.

Contents

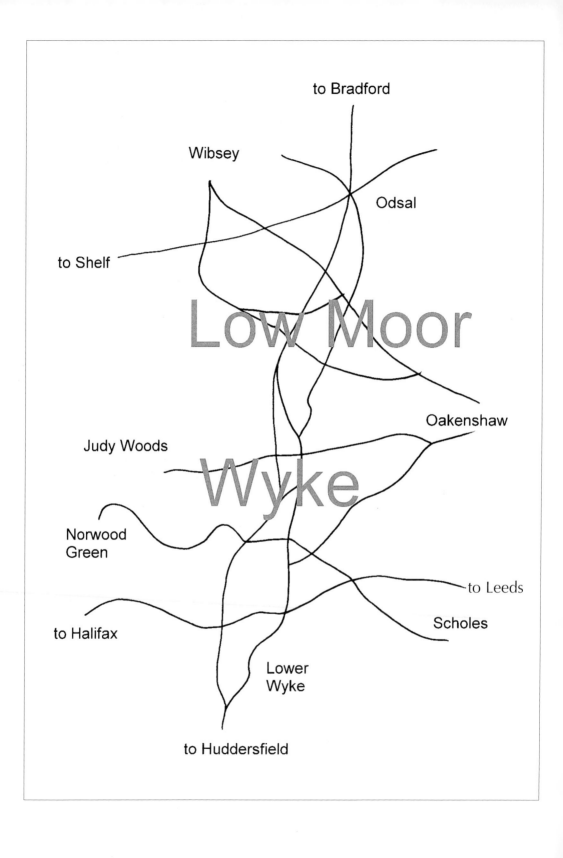

Acknowledgements

We wish to thank members and friends of Low Moor Local History Group, Wyke Local History Group, the churches of Low Moor and Wyke, and the Friends of Judy Woods, who have so generously let us use their photographs. Special thanks are due to Graham Hall, who gave us unrestricted access to his collection of old postcards. We acknowledge the help of Bradford Libraries Local Studies Department in allowing us to reproduce the aerial photographs of Wyke.

Foreword

I am pleased and proud to introduce this book, compiled by the Low Moor and Wyke Local History groups. A few years ago I read *Wike*, by the same group, since Wyke was where our small family weaving mill, Barraclough & Co. was founded in 1892 by my great-grandfather, Benjamin (1848-1921). I still remember its telephone number: Low Moor 53.

Recently I was looking at a copy of *Bradford Fifty Years Ago*, published in 1897, a book that once belonged to Samuel Wright of 'The Griffe', Wyke, but there is no mention in it of Judy North, of Judy Woods fame. I must confess, however, to an early interest in 'Judy', since it was my pet name in childhood.

My father had lived in Wyke as a child but during the First World War the family moved from Wyke to Hipperholme, though Great Uncle Cyril still lived there, on Green Lane. My grandfather and father went to their work by train, one stop along from Lightcliffe. From a bedroom window I could see Wyke Church on its hill, over a mile away. The mill itself was only about 500 yards from the edge of the 'Low Wood' part of Judy Woods. From Lightcliffe, though, we walked to 'Judy Bridge' via Norwood Green.

I read later in one of J. Horsfall Turner's invaluable local histories that the ancient forest of Bryanscholes once covered most of this area. Perhaps a Mr Rookes of Royds Hall added to what was already there by planting beeches? Royds Hall was just a little too far away for a comfortable walk, but I liked Judy Woods best of all our destinations, loved the beeches and the bluebells and the whole 'feel' of the place. As a child I did not know the separate names of the various woods, and I don't believe my family did either. The beck that ran through Royds Hall Great Wood marked the boundary between the old parishes of Halifax and Bradford, and is now the boundary between Calderdale and Bradford.

I did not know then that we were walking over land that many of my direct Barraclough ancestors had cultivated. For two hundred years, from the early seventeenth to the end of the eighteenth century, they had farmed in and around Horse Close; Richard Barraclough, baptised 1546, 'of Norwoodgrene' in the first Halifax Parish Register, is my direct ancestor.

To me as a child, Judy Woods did seem 'home'. As well as family walks we children would cycle there in those happy days when it was safe to roam around all day 'playing out'. In my imagination the woods are always bathed in sunlight, and I see them now through the enchanted looking-glass of childhood memory. Those haunts symbolise in a special way 'The Past'. I'd love to be magically transported back to both that time and that place.

June Barraclough
(Author of *The Heart of the Rose* and *Rooks Nest*)

Introduction

In its heyday in the 1800s the town of Bradford was the centre of the worsted industry. To the south of the town, and at that time not part of the borough, were the villages of Low Moor and Wyke. Until the later years of the eighteenth century they were sparsely populated, with the majority of people employed on the land. Low Moor was the name given to the area of moorland and scrub below the small village of Wibsey, which occupied the high ground between the 'bowl' containing the town of Bradford to the north and the Spen Valley to the south.

In 1788 the bankrupt Lord of the Manor of Wibsey, Edward Rookes Leeds, committed suicide. A group of men (who would eventually form the Low Moor Company) purchased much of his land for the mineral rights. In the 1790s a forge was built on the marshy ground known as Black Syke and several communities grew around it, including Raw Nook, Wesley Place, Hill Top and Moorside. Together they were known as Low Moor, and as part of the Township of North Bierley they became part of Bradford in 1899, along with Wyke.

Wyke was in the parish of Birstall, situated on the road between Coley and Scholes, and until the coming of the turnpike road from Bradford to Huddersfield, despite its close proximity, it was not easily directly accessible from Low Moor.

This selection of photographs has been assembled by Geoff and Mary Twentyman of Low Moor Local History Group and Peter Walker and Maureen Barstow of Wyke Local History Group.

The Wyke Local History Group was formed in 1994 and meets on the first Thursday evening of the month, with guest speakers on various topics.

The group has produced one book, *Wike, Where They're All Alike* (now out of print), four calendars, a plate commemorating 100 years of Wyke being incorporated into Bradford and a one-hour video of the interesting and historic buildings and features of the area.

The two main achievements of the group have been successfully campaigning for the school tower to be registered as a Class II listed building when the school was in danger of closing, and the return to the village of an ancient mile/guide post which had been removed to a museum in Bradford several years ago.

Low Moor Local History Group was founded in 1995 and meets on the first Friday afternoon of each month; topics covered include local and more general historical subjects.

The group has published two books about the area. *Low Moor, the Beginning of a Journey* (£6.00 including p&p) by the late Norman Ellis, which describes his early life there in the 1920s, and *Around and About Low Moor* (£7.00 including p&p), a compilation of photographs and memories by group members. Both books are available from LMLHG, 13 St Abbs Fold, Odsal, Bradford, BD6 1EL.

Those interested in Low Moor can also explore the area's history on the internet, by visiting John Nicholl's site at http://www.ngfl.ac.uk/wards/lowmoorschool/history/lowmoor/index.html.

one

School
Days

Carr Lane Primary School bus trip, 1946. This was the first school outing after the end of the Second World War. Trips were suspended during the war.

Carr Lane School in the early twentieth century. It was built by the Low Moor Company in 1863. The fields behind the school are now occupied by the Markfield estate. The then notable black and white chimney at the ironworks can be seen to the right of the tall chimney near the centre of the photograph. The school buildings are now occupied by a meat products company.

New Works School, Low Moor.

Everyone who takes their rubbish to the waste disposal site in Low Moor passes this building, the former New Works School, at the junction of Dealburn Road and New Works Road. It is now occupied by a car dealer, but was built as a school in 1872 by the Low Moor Company, and after the explosion at the munitions site in 1916 was used as a mortuary.

Many generations of former pupils have happy memories of the present Hill Top Infant School, but there are still some old scholars around who can recall attending this building, which was demolished following a fire to make way for the new school in 1926. According to the local historian James Parker it was originally erected as a chapel by the Primitive Methodists, possibly in the 1830s, then used as the village school before becoming a church school.

Hill Top School, 1949. From left to right, back row: Miss Gertrude Hirst, Gordon Allen, Jack Ward, Terry Rhodes, Jack Mahoney, Leslie Smith, Peter Helliwell, Barrie Cliffe, Michael D'Agnostino. Middle row: Michael Hardisty, John Benn, Brian Lake, Bernard Harper, Eric Butterfield, John Goldsborough, Eddie Wood, David Glover, Jimmy Laycock, Stephen Benn. Front row: Margaret Firth, Wendy Elliott, Audrey Lightowlers, Marion Binns, Joan Battye, Maureen Bentley, Beryl Pullan, Anthea Tulip, Maureen Mears, Jean Sheddon, Mary Flintoff.

Above: Three little misses of the early 1950s make sure that their hands are nice and clean for the next lesson at Raw Nook School. From left to right: Joan Laycock, Susan Whitaker, Hazel Lightowler.

Left: The building in Cleckheaton Road, which now houses Old School Mews, was built by the Low Moor Company in 1814 and became known locally as 'Scott's' as a result of the long period of headships by a father and son of that name. This is Joseph Scott, schoolmaster from 1882 to 1900, who followed his father John Scott, who had held the post since 1838, a total of sixty-two years.

Scott's School – standard 3A – 1957. From left to right, back row: Stephen Naylor, David Needham, Max Bradford, Christopher Haxby, Ian Sutcliffe, Cyril Stinchcombe, Alan Hudson, Michael Woodward, Colin Speight, Ian Stothers, Geoffrey Twentyman, Roy Thompson. Third row: Peggy Sherlock, Elaine Spencer, Denise Lake, Susan Firth, Jacqueline Hodgson, Elaine Robinson, Wendy Warnett, Andrea Blackburn, Christine Nelmes, Joyce Bailey, David Lumb, Miss Sowden. Second row: Sandra Dobson, Rona Booth, Linda Jones, Sandra Thomas, Audrey Megson, Doreen Hanson, Christine Brough, Sandra Merrin, Joan Ormiston, Linda Rhodes, Sandra Gascoigne, Averil Small. Front row: Roger Coverdale, John Barker, Stuart Holden, Peter Harrison, Malcolm Elliot, Leslie Collinson, Graham Charlesworth, Allan Wilson, Raymond Kershaw, Terry Maleham.

Opposite above: Scott's School pupils, *c.* 1937.

Opposite below: Scott's School pupils of the early 1950s. From left to right, back row: –?–, Bobby Pearson, Stuart Newton, Ann Pearson, Susan Ackroyd, Carolyn Jennings, Jean Anderson, Joan Laycock, –?–, David Charlesworth, –?–, Miss Sowden (later Mrs Thompson). Middle row: Jean Wadsworth, Christine Jagger, –?–, Doreen Briggs, Maureen Boocock, Cynthia Smales, –?–, Maureen O'Neil, –?–, –?–, Front row: –?–, –?–, Alan Walker, –?–, Alan Goldsmith, –?–, Keith Brear.

This key was used at the opening ceremony of Wyke Board School in 1904 when aldermen and councillors of Bradford attended the ceremony. Obviously it was not used after the occasion, but has been retained and presented to the Wyke Local History Group.

Pupils and their parents make their way home from the new Wyke Board School, *c.* 1906. The buildings are now used by Wyke Community College. Note the newsagent's hut, which was replaced by a sturdier building in the 1980s.

Wyke Board School orchestra, *c.* 1906, only two years after the school opened. It is believed that one of these pupils was Leslie Heward, who conducted the Birmingham Philharmonic Orchestra in the 1930s and '40s. He died in the 1940s at the height of his career in music. The headmaster of the school was Mr Walter Smith (standing on the right). Wyke was a working-class area, but it should be noted how well these children are dressed.

Wyke Infant School, May Day 1946. The photograph was taken on Wyke recreation ground. To the left of the swings, the remains of the air-raid shelter are apparent. The May King is John Bartle, and the May Queen is Judith Brinnand. Other names recalled include John Dace, Terence Tailford, David Briggs, Alan Heaton, David Bullock, Euan Pearson (in satin suit), David Ingham and Ernest Stocks.

In the 1950s there was a reorganisation of the schools in Wyke and, pending the building of Wyke Manor School and the conversion of the secondary school into premises for the junior school, various Sunday Schools were used for classes. This picture shows a class, together with their headmaster Mr Creasey and teacher Mrs Hird, outside the Methodist Sunday School. From left to right, back row: Edward Barraclough, John Broomhead, Karl Satloka, William Clayton, Nelson Kershaw. Second row: Leonard Harvey, John Gleeson, Graham Ingham, Colin Broadley, Douglas Stockley, Michael Kaye. Third row: Jane Rhodes, Elaine Sharp, Christine Ashington, Anne Timperley, Doreen Pearson, Patricia Kelly, Christine Rathbone, Julie Lemmon, Front row: Tony Clark, Catherine Donnelly, Angela Coleman, Jennifer Dawson, Brenda Hill, Brenda Wilson, Jacqueline Cooper, Graham Locker.

Opposite above: Wyke Church of England Infant School, *c.* 1926. From left to right, back row: Harry Kellett, Harry Holdsworth, Frank Drake, Tom Inman, John Morton, Leonard Eckershall. Third row: Frank Sugden, William Bland, Arthur Smith, Frank Snary, Frank Spencer, Olga Lee, Mary Harlow, ? Williams, Tom Woodhead. Second row: Dorothy Dawson, Jane Percival, Vera Emmett, Marjorie Jagger, Marjorie Littlewood, Margaret Marshall, Hilda Kellett. Front row: Mary Bond, Mary Shaw, Mary Eastwood, Vera Thornton, Mary Horner, Lottie Bottomley.

Opposite below: Wyke Council Infant School, 1932. This is the year when the pupils in the oldest class in the infant school were transferred to Carr Lane School for their education up to 'scholarship' time. This is the first class to have been moved in this way. From left to right, back row: Lily Wilson, Mary English, Joan Bennett, Jean Tordoff, Jean Wolsey, Margaret Holdsworth, Betty Ellis, Winnie Hartley, Annie F. Smith. Fourth row: Marion Horsley, Mary Thornton, Annie Sharp, Beryl Armitage, Joyce Tacey, Marion Hanson, Jean Jordan, Evelyn Douglas, Maureen Ward, Irene Williams, Lily Harbottle, Edward Wilks. Third row: Vera Kellett, Margaret Bostock, Annie Firth, Barbara Brayshaw, Joan Hanson, Evelyn Jagger, Lilian Malone, Enid Speight, Joyce Ramsden, Douglas Gaines, Eddie Lister. Second row: -?-, Victor Jagger, Peter Wilkinson. Front row: Leslie Healey, Alan Ambrose, Walter Bond, Basil Hirst, Donald Ackroyd, Sydney Bond, Billie Greenwood, Donald Wright.

A class of boys at Wyke National School on 4 October 1906. Classes were held for many years in this former school building, which is situated at the top of Green Lane. The school was closed for use after the Low Moor Explosion in 1916, when much of the local property was damaged or affected by movement of foundations. In more recent times it has been used as a Sunday School by St Mary's Church, a base for Wyke Christian Fellowship youth activities and latterly as a community centre.

A class from Wyke Infant School in the early 1900s. The classes look smart in white collars, pinafores and sailor suits. Was this usual dress or for the benefit of the photographer?

two

Holidays

The young boys and girls, in two discrete groups outside Harold Park gates, may have indulged in the social activity of 'promming' inside the park in a few years time. 'Promming' (or promenading) was a particular summer Sunday's activity when groups of young ladies would stroll up and down the park, with young men initially looking on and then perhaps joining them. An innocent activity somewhat removed from today's nightclubbing generation! One might normally expect park gate pillars to be made of stone, but here in Low Moor they are, of course, made of iron!

The grand monument, with drinking fountains, erected in memory of Harold Gathorne Hardy, after whom the park is named. The building situated in the background cannot be recalled within anyone's living memory. It may have been used to house the boats, prior to the days when they were stored overnight on the island.

The level of Harold Park lake looks quite low in this 1930s scene. The boatman's hut and the landing stage are now long gone – as are the boats themselves. 'Come in number nine – your time is up – oh dear, are you in difficulties number six?' The greenhouses were demolished in more recent years when the Council reorganised its plant-rearing activities.

The ornate Fountain Pond in Harold Park, near the Cemetery Road gates, was later reduced in status to a paddling pool and eventually filled in and grassed over.

The Harold Park bowling team pose proudly with their trophy on a summer's day in the late 1940s. From left to right, back row: -?-, Harrison Walker, Jack Gledhill (?). Middle row: Clifford Padgett, Joe Haigh, -?-, Jack Emmett, Percy Ellis, Wright Bottomley, -?-, Tommy Howard, Harold (Gerry) Wilman, ? Smith. Front row: Donald Haigh, Walter Stead, Sam Sutcliffe, Walter Crabtree, Charles Henry, ? Sykes, Bernard Harper.

Low Moor Wesleyan AFC, 1921/22. The group was photographed by the entrance to the Wesley Place Sunday School on First Street. The manse can be seen over the wall in the background.

Unfortunately we do not know the identities of these champion billiard players from the Harold Club in 1912. The large plaque is the Moorhouse Shield, awarded at the Bradford Charity Billiards Tournament.

No details are known of this gentlemanly cricket team (and supporters), but it just had to be included in this collection! It is possible that the picture was taken on the former cricket ground adjacent to Royds Hall. The card on which the photograph is mounted reads 'F. Smith, Harold Park Art Studio, Low Moor Nr Bradford'. The studio was situated near the top of Park Road.

HAROLD PARK   SPORTS & GALA

The carnival procession makes its way up School Street. The cart to the left carries rolls of cloth and the small cart to the right might have belonged to an ice cream seller. Many of the ladies seem to be sporting spectacular hats. Had they been made especially for the occasion?

Opposite above: No wonder the Holy Trinity cricket team of 1934 look proud of themselves; they had won the cup, the league and the evening league. Left to right (non-players): G. Spencely, W. Holden, H. Oates, E. Mawson, Revd R. Broadbent, W. Pyrah, W. Eastwood, W. Eastwood's son. Back row (players): A. Tetley, M. Sutcliffe, J. Terry, T. Tetley, J. Blamires. Middle row: F. Shackleton, P. Nudds, H. Ellis (captain), F. Tetley, W. Binns. Front row: W. Mounsey, N. Cooper. Boys: J. Nudds, W. Eastwood's son.

Opposite below: This print was taken from a sepia photograph and is marked 'Harold Park – Sports and Gala'. It is a reminder that the main purpose of the gala was to raise money to support the Bradford hospital services in the years before the National Health Service came into existence. Now there's an idea…!

The message on top of the coal cart reads 'Order Crigglestone Haigh Moor cobbles and nuts', but one can tell from the finery on the horses that ordinary deliveries have been suspended and they are bound for Harold Park and the gala. The photograph was taken in Bolton Street. Many older residents will remember Mitchell's shoe shop at the top of the street and the Furnace Inn half way down. The photograph is embossed 'Woodcock Wibsey'.

A postcard from Wyke Local History Group's collection. Local carriers with horses in tandem and full harness – Wyke traders and residents also took part in the Low Moor Gala.

All eyes were on Edna Priestley on this occasion in 1936. She had just been elected the Low Moor Carnival Queen for the year. From left to right: Eileen Bryden, Elsie Dobson, Leonora Stead, Margery Shaw, Dorothy Leach, Lillian Shaw.

The Low Moor Carnival Queen, most likely the following year, 1937, when Edna (as the previous year's queen) hands over to her successor Annie Butterworth. From left to right: Joyce Richardson, -?-, Edna Priestley, Annie Butterworth, Betty Rowley, -?-, -?-, Gabrielle Fairburn, -?-.

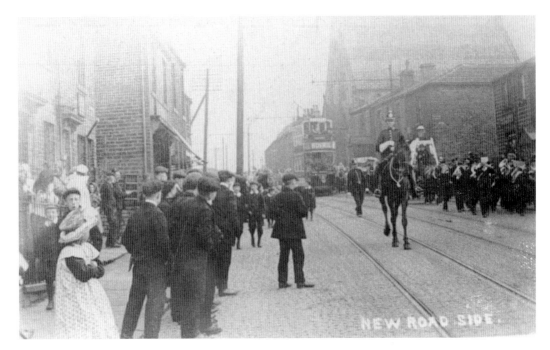

The Low Moor Gala parade commenced at the Robin Hood and Little John Inn on the green at Wyke and proceeded through the village via Towngate and New Road Side, and forward to Low Moor. A mounted policeman escorts the parade along New Road Side and ensures the tram keeps its distance in this shot taken prior to, or just after, the First World War.

The 'wagon train' has halted outside the Robin Hood and Little John public house on Wyke Green. An ideal place – grass for the horses – pub for the people – shops close by! The barn on the right has been converted to a dining area and music room. To the right of the old barn was a bowling green. Originally built in 1704, it is reputed to have some connection with the outlaw Robin Hood – hence the name.

Wyke Temperance Band was formed in 1859 as a flute and pipe band and converted to brass soon after. It then rivalled Wyke Old Band (which went out of existence in 1890) in various contests. Both were 'crack' bands but Temperance emerged as the better one and lasted until the Second World War. It won the Belle Vue Open Championship in 1888, 1889 and 1898. The principal cornet player was Jeremiah Holdsworth, whose daughter, Phyllis, is now (in 2005) one hundred years old. She lived in Wyke until recently moving into a rest home. This postcard is franked '10.00 a.m. 23 Dec.' and although the year is illegible it carries an Edward VII stamp. Addressed to Fred Hind Esq. at City Shed, Wyke, the band's secretary L. Pollard confirms their intention to wait upon him on Monday next and play seasonable music.

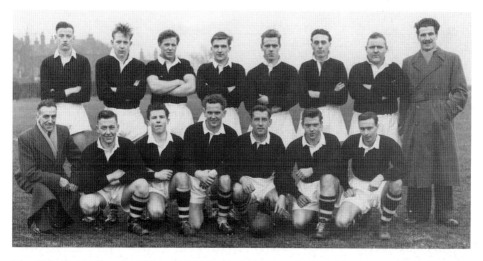

The Wyke Rugby League Club, established over 100 years ago, has attained success in Bradford and Yorkshire competitions with many players being signed by professional clubs. Here is the team of 1955/56 – winners of Bradford's league and cup. From left to right, back row: Brian Carter, Dave Butterworth, Keith Wilkinson, Bill Waterworth, Pete Barraclough, Dougie McLean, Ronnie Lockwood, Gordon French (committee). Front row: Harry McLean (committee), Jack Greenough, Alan Lee, Nicky Newton, Bill Towler (captain), Colin Rhodes, Derek Lilley. This photograph was taken in February 1956 when they drew 5-5 in the Yorkshire Cup. When the game was replayed at Redhill the following week, Wyke won 15-14.

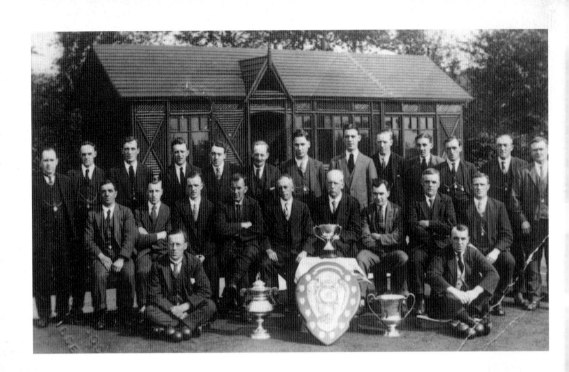

Here are Wyke Ladies Bowling Club in 1969, the winners of the Afternoon League Championship of the Bradford Ladies Bowling Association. From left to right, back row: Mrs L. Tabrah, Mrs M. Jagger, Mrs M. Gallemore, Mrs B. Worsnop. Front row: Mrs K. Jones, Mrs W. Mallinson, Mrs M. Booth, Miss I. Smith, Mrs A. Jowett.

Opposite above: The golden years of Wyke Bowling Club – winners of the Bradford Parks Goodwin League in 1918, 1919, 1922, 1925, 1926 and 1928, plus the Howarth Cup in 1922, and in 1926 the Yorkshire Brotherton Cup, the Yorkshire Charity Cup and the Yorkshire Championship Shield. Members in 1926, from left to right, back row: W. Bottomley, H. Rhodes, W. Shaw, H. Shaw, F. Firth, A.E. Harrison, H. Stott, W. Smith, J. Holdsworth, J.N. Jones, S. Rhodes, F. Healey, W. Webster. Middle row: J.W. Shooter, A. Jones, H. Kellett, S. Jagger, J. Carr (captain), W. Smith, H. Smith (vice-captain), L. Brook, J. Chadwick Front row: W. Hargreaves, J.E. Jagger.

Opposite below: Wyke Ladies Bowling Club in the 1940s. From left to right, back row: Mrs Greenwood, Mrs Ramsden, Freda Wilkinson, Ida Smith, K. Jones, M. Robinson, V. Ormonroyd, Mrs Bell. Front row: Mrs Stokes, Mrs Lindsey, V. Jagger, B. Worsnop, E. Howard, Mrs Forrest, -?- , Mrs Tordoff, Mrs Brook, Mrs Mallinson.

Cricket was another pleasant way of spending Saturday afternoons and summer evenings. The clubs in Wyke were formed by the churches – the Temperance Mission, Westfield Church and the Moravian Church – and the Liberal Club. Here are two line-ups from Wyke Temperance Cricket Club, *c.* 1950. In this photograph the team, wearing caps, poses with some club officials. From left to right, back row: S. Northen, A. Fellows, G. Pearson, R. Griffiths, C. Rhodes, K. Hirst, D. Woodcock, G. Boughton, A. Broadley. Front row: T. Rhodes, H. Holdsworth, N. Kellett, L. Crowther, R. Kellett, D. Roebuck, J. Roebuck.

Wyke Temperance Cricket Club are winners of the Roberts Cup. From left to right, back row: D. Illingworth, E. Brown, W. Sugden, C. Rhodes, L. Kellett, C. Dargue. Front row: W. Berry, J. Wainwright, J. Bentley, J. Irvine, N. Kellett, R. Kellett.

Moravian Church cricket team, winners of the Bradford and District Mutual Sunday School League Division 'C', 1957. From left to right, back row: R. Kellett, P. Day, B. Clark, G. Mallinson, P. Greenhough, D. Seymour. Front row: T. Rastick, K. Ingham, P. Walker, T. Ellis, H. Jowett.

A group of Wyke tradesmen enjoying their annual outing, *c.* 1940. The Greyhound Inn was obviously a stop en route to enjoy some liquid refreshment.

Above: Majorettes taking part in the British Legion Garden Party, which was held in 1934 in the cricket ground at Royds Hall. From left to right, back row: Kathleen Benn, Iris Warren, Margaret Bailey, Maureen Ward, -?-, Jean Jordan, Winnie Smalley, Mary Eastwood. Front row: -?-, Doreen Warren, Joyce Richardson, -?- , Annie Firth, Renee Byford, Margaret Boyes, Joyce Smalley.

A crowd looks on as trophies are presented at the Wyke Horticultural Society Show, some time in the 1950s. John Willie Shooter is stood on the left wearing a bow tie.

Opposite below: Members of the Wyke Townswomen's Guild 'planting a tree in '73' in the garden of Wyke Library. From left to right, front row: Lorna Farrar, Estelle Foster, Mabel Bennett, Margaret Callaway, Mollie Foster, David Croft (Bradford Libraries), Elsie Howard (chairman), Maureen Barstow, Kathleen Shaw, Alma Jowett.

Looking towards Mayfield Avenue, with no sign of Prospect Mills yet. There was plenty of room for a stroll on the promenade and to enjoy the flowerbeds, with music provided from the bandstand. This was transferred from Horton Park in 1902 but was dismantled after only a few years.

Another view of the park showing the bandstand and another structure, possibly a shelter. In this view we are looking towards Worthing Head Road.

The bowling green features on this postcard from the 1930s. If you look carefully you can see the netting around the tennis courts, which are now no more.

Over the years local children have taken advantage of the facilities in the recreation ground, including the kiddies' play corner. The chimney of Prospect Mills is in the background.

Although this postcard is captioned 'In Wyke Woods 2' we would call them Judy Woods. This is High Fernley Road on a sunny Edwardian day. Old Hannah Woods, with its old mine workings, are to the left and Low Wood is to the right.

On the same part of High Fernley Road a couple are enjoying a trip in a pony and trap. This part of the road is often very muddy and the wall to the right has been replaced by a less aesthetically pleasing metal fence. The 'Friends of Judy Woods' are currently involved in repairing the dry-stone walling in this part of the woods.

This intriguing picture only came to light again recently. It was made by the wet collodion method, which was the standard photographic process for a time between the 1850s and the 1870s. It involved the use of a thick glass plate on which to create a negative, which was exposed in the camera with the emulsion still wet. The old lady is almost certainly Judy North, from whom Judy Woods take their name. She died in 1870 aged seventy-five, so this image must date from the late 1860s.

Following the death of her third husband, Joseph North, in 1850 Judy and her son from her first marriage, John Barraclough, took over the running of the North's family's "pleasure gardens." Judy sold ginger beer and parkin pig to visitors to the gardens. We don't know the identity of the man.

Both of these prints were discovered by Peter Harrison among the effects of his late father Percy, who had a photographer's shop in Little Horton. It was labelled 'Son O'Judy and his drinking pals'. Again it's not John Barraclough. Look closely; these men, dressed in their Sunday best, are relaxing at a table and partaking of ginger bread and ginger beer. Could they be Judy's customers?

Here's Judy Bridge, or Horse Close Bridge as it is more properly known. The stream through Judy Woods marks the boundary between Bradford and Calderdale. The land in the foreground, formerly used for Scout camps, is now overgrown with brambles and bracken. The field on the far side of the bridge is where the North family had their 'public gardens' from the 1840s until the 1860s. Judy North's cottage was probably at the back of the field, off a short lane leading from High Fernley Road. A geophysical survey is being carried out in 2005 for the Friends of Judy Woods to try to find the exact position of the house.

In the early years of the twentieth century the stream below Judy Bridge seems to have had just the same attraction for young boys as it does today.

This postcard is marked 5 September 1905 and a gentleman in uniform (a policeman?) has climbed down the side of the bridge to pose for the photographer.

Could this be a Sunday School outing to Judy Bridge? The children seem to be in their best clothes and again the stream is attracting their attention. This picture is taken from the other side of the bridge to the previous one. The fine old ash tree helps to date photographs of the bridge, and it is still thriving today.

WATERFALL JUDY WOODS   XLCR Nº 4

Left: This waterfall is probably the one down at the bottom of Low Wood, but the banks have eroded somewhat in the past ninety years or so and the saplings have grown to maturity.

Below: Lots of people mistakenly think this cabin, from which refreshments were sold in the 1950s, was connected with Judy. However, she traded at the bridge one hundred years before. It's still a popular spot but alas no refreshments can be purchased nowadays.

three

Holy
Days

Only the graveyard of Wesley Place Wesleyan Church can be seen today from this viewpoint on Chapel Road, off Cleckheaton Road. The building in the centre with eight windows visible is the first chapel erected on this site in 1808, at a cost of £1,500. It was demolished to make way for the new chapel, which opened in 1905. The portion with the chimney to the right was the vestry, and the cottage at the extreme right was the caretaker and sexton's house. The building to the left with the spire was the Sunday School erected, in 1877. The gravestones, now somewhat neglected, contain some useful information for family and local historians. The monumental inscriptions were transcribed by Arthur Blackburn in the 1920s and can be consulted at Bradford Library.

The interior of the old Wesleyan Church at Wesley Place, demolished in 1905. When originally built it could seat 640 but by the time this photograph was taken, shortly before demolition, it had been altered several times and could seat almost 800. The organ was added in 1862 and the double-decker pulpit had been replaced by this rostrum and choir stall in the 1880s. The door at the top right connected the building to the Sunday School. The stone from the old chapel was used in the building of the terrace of houses on Chapel Road, one of which was the caretaker's house.

BRADFORD LOW MOOR.

New Wesleyan Church.

THE

Memorial Stones

WILL BE PLACED IN POSITION ON

Saturday, June 25th, 1904.

— 2 · 30 —

For Programme, see Pages 2 and 3.

IMMEDIATELY AFTER THE CEREMONY,

TEA will be provided in a MARQUEE and in WESLEY SCHOOL.

TICKETS, 1/- EACH. TO BE FOLLOWED BY

A Thanksgiving Meeting

Chair to be taken at 6.30 by

← Mr. ABRAHAM WOODHEAD.

CHIEF SPEAKERS

Rev. SILVESTER WHITEHEAD

President-Elect of the Wesleyan Methodist Conference.

Rev. D. A. De MOUILPIED,

BIRMINGHAM.

Special Collection for the Building Fund.

Friends who cannot be present are earnestly desired to send the largest Financial Help in their power to the Pastor—Rev. GEORGE ADCOCK, The Manse, LOW MOOR, in order to enable him to complete the £1,016 which, at the Valedictory Services in the Old Church, he pledged himself to raise in connection with the Stone-Laying Ceremony. ☞ P.T.O

The front page of the programme for the dedication of the memorial stones at the new Wesleyan Church on 25 June 1904.

Mr John Hirst, a leading member of New Road Side Wesleyan chapel, Wyke, lays a memorial stone on their behalf at the new chapel. Mr Hirst was the manager of the saw mill and the wright's shop for the Low Moor Company, and as such lived in the first of the cottages on Abb Scott, which is now a kennels. At the time the photograph was taken he would have been eighty-five years of age.

47

Right: The new Wesleyan Methodist Church, First Street, opened on 7 May 1905. It was described as being in the Italianate style. It cost approximately £7,000. The copper dome would be a landmark until the church's demise in 1959. The dome actually suffered some damage in the explosion at the munitions factory in 1916, but it wasn't until someone . went on the roof in the late 1930s that the damage was noticed!

Below: The interior of the new church.

This is the wedding of Eleanor Carter and Percy William Breaks on 13 July 1906, and is thought to be outside the last house on Railway Terrace, Raw Nook. From left to right, front row: -?-, groom, bride, Edith Woodhead, -?-. Row behind bride: to her right, Samuel Carter (father), to her left, Mary Elizabeth Dobson. Two rows behind and immediately above, Lydia Carter (mother). On steps: Herbert Dobson.

The marriage certificate for the above wedding. It looks a very grand affair but Percy was a railway goods clerk and Eleanor was a dressmaker. No doubt she was responsible for creating those impressive dresses.

Children from various Low Moor schools on an Ascension Day in the late 1940s.

The predecessors of the 'Tiller Girls' as they appeared at the Raw Nook Sunday School pantomime in 1948. From left to right, back row: Norah Varley, Pat Lightowlers, Joyce Tiffany, Jean Butterworth, Edna Linas, Jean Kasher, Audrey Ellis, Rena Linas.

The cast of *Our Silver Wedding*, a Yorkshire dialect play written and produced by Fred
Crowther at Oxley Place in the 1930s. From left to right, back row: Edith Annie Drake,
Renie Smith, May Slicer, Annie Ellis, Doris Learoyd, Hilda Crowther, Mabel Sugden.
Middle row: Elsie Briggs, Ida Smith, Alice Sugden, Alice Crowther, Mary Jane Norton, -?-,
May Crowther. Front row: Elsie Ward, Alan Sugden, John Sugden (?), -?-, Fred Crowther.

A Sunday School party from Wesley Place Church about to set off from Main Street on
the Whitsuntide Walk in 1953. The information on the cart indicates that it was supplied
courtesy of Mr Hughes of Seed Farm, Buttershaw. The farm made way for part of the
Woodside housing estate in the 1950s. From left to right, back row: Annie Bransby, Pat
Dobson, Betty Knight. Middle row: Ian Cuthbertson, Philip Megson, Audrey Megson,
David Hirst, John Downes, Bessie Glover. Front line: Geoffrey Holden, David Fuller,
Michael Acton, Stuart Holden, June Wheatley, Pamela Cuthbertson.

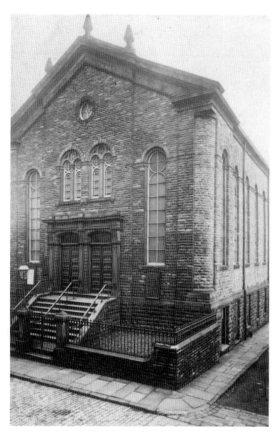

Left: The Primitive Methodist chapel in School Street was erected in 1870 and was flanked appropriately by James Street and John Street. It replaced an earlier building next door which was then converted into cottages. Gradual structural faults resulted in a spectacular collapse of the frontage in April 1947. Fortunately no one was injured. The members were offered the permanent use of Oxley Place Sunday School and the building was adapted as business premises until its demolition in the 1970s.

Below: 'Worship the Lord in the beauty of holiness' proclaims the text on the wall inside School Street chapel. The basic decorations and furnishings appear to complement the 'primitive' theme. However, spiritual warmth and many well-loved social activities could be found there.

Ladies at the School Street chapel bazaar in the 1930s. From left to right, back row: Mrs Exon, Mrs Stobart, Mrs Jennings, -?-, Aggie Stead, -?-, Polly Ellis, -?-, Mrs Brydon, Mabel Firth. Middle row: -?-, Minnie Priestley, ? Knowles, Mrs Adams, Elsie Stobart, Rachel Taylor, Emily Bateman, -?-. Front row: Elsie Kellett, Brian Jennings (?), Lily Kellett, Emma Bateman, -?-, Verena Coy, Dorothy Priestley.

The cast of a production at School Street chapel in the 1930s. From left to right, back row: Ethel Stead, -?-, Wilfred Bryden, Norman Ellis, Albert Bateman, Harry Fox. Middle row: Eliza Ford, -?-, Lily Pearson, -?-, Agnes Barraclough , -?-. Front row: Dorothy Priestley, Verena Coy, Eileen Bryden, Elsie Dobson, Nellie Priestley.

The Ranter Revellers of School Street Methodist chapel, 1930 ('Ranters' was a nickname for the Primitive Methodist denomination). From left to right, back row: Brian Horsfall, Irvine Barraclough, Evelyn Hardy, John (Jack) S. Hardy, Ida Best, Sidney Jelfs, Bertha Priestley. Front row: Albert Pearson, Agnes Barraclough, William Barraclough, Doris Adams, Willie Firth.

The young ladies of Oxley Place after their production of *Aladdin and Out* in the late 1940s. From left to right, back row: Vera Neale, Dorothy Priestley, May Moody, Ethel Stead, Myra Batty, Mrs Johnson. Middle row: Betty Eastwood, Nellie Priestley, Verena Coy, Eileen Bryden. Between Rows: Evelyn Ellis. Front row: Kathleen Stead, Mavis Neale, Edna Priestley, Agnes Barraclough.

The stone over the front doorway of Oxley Place Wesleyan Methodist Sunday School on School Street, proclaimed that it was 're-built in 1859'. A plaque over the rear door stated it was actually built in 1844 and enlarged in 1847. The land was given by Dr Samuel Oxley.

In April 1947 the frontage of School Street Methodist chapel collapsed leaving the congregation without a place of worship. The members of Wesley Place Church offered them Oxley Place Sunday School, the upstairs of which was converted into a church whilst the downstairs became their Sunday School. Next door was Martin's Bank, later taken over by Barclays Bank.

Oxley Place Sunday School children who collected for the JMA (Juvenile Missionary Association), c. 1950. From left to right, back row: Edith Sugden (JMA secretary), Mavis Neale, Stanley Garnett, Dennis Wilson, Joan Stobart, Katherine Kellett, John Sugden, David Cooper, Raymond Barraclough, Eric Smith, Beverley Hardy. Middle row: Christopher Shackleton, June Osborne, -?-, -?-, Maureen Woodhead, Jennifer Wilkinson, Godfrey Ledder, Mavis Eyles. Front row: -?-, -?-, -?-, -?-, Shirley Eyles, Ian Cowling.

Oxley Place Sunday School scholars of the mid-1960s. From left to right, back row: Stephen Wynn, Philip Paley, Adrian Jagger, David Wynn, Martin Arnold, Judith Murgatroyd, -?-, -?-. Middle row: Susan Walton, -?-, -?-, Elaine Broadbent, -?-, Helen Woodhead, Dorothy Paley, -?-, Kathryn Murgatroyd. Front row: Katherine Butterfield, -?-, Lynda Butterworth, David Arnold, Derek Arnold, Leslie Butterfield, Trevor Murgatroyd.

Albert Street Wesleyan Reform chapel was erected on land off Manor Row in 1879 but, because of its corrugated iron roof, it was known by all locally as 'tin chapel'. It was replaced by the present church, further along Manor Row, in 1928. The Wesleyan Reform Sunday School anniversary was held (weather permitting) in the field adjacent to the chapel. A 'grandstand' platform was erected against the adjoining warehouse. The landlord of the nearby New Inn provided seating for his customers outside so they could combine their regular pleasure with the annual event!

This is the inside of the 'tin chapel' at their Harvest Festival. Grapes and bananas hang from the walls and turnips and cabbages are balancing precariously on the top of the platform. There seems to be specially baked bread in appropriate shapes and sheaves of corn at the centre front.

Pageant of Noble Womanhood at Wesleyan Reform chapel, 1934. Left to right, back row: Nellie White, -?-, Marion Colbert, Bessie Rayner, Alice Cursley, Mrs Sykes, Marion Wilkinson. Fourth row: Alice Firth, -?-, Susan Stead, -?-, -?-, Lilian Woodhouse, Marion Barraclough, Emily Blagborough, Mrs E. Dean, Martha Wright, Mrs Richardson, Mary Seed. Third row: Minnie Furness, Nellie Mallinson, Lily Wilkinson, Mrs Surbuts, Phyllis Wood, Nellie Blackburn, Mrs Rowley, Mary Bowman, Amelia Asquith, Mrs Colbert, Ivy Ackroyd, Nellie Surbuts, Mary Ackroyd. Second row: -?-, -?-, Frances Fairburn, Cissie Thornton, Lilian Holden, Hilda Butterworth, Ethel Kellett, Mrs Birkby, Mrs Jagger, Louie Kellett, Ethel Gibson. Front row: Mary Jagger, Walter Birkby, Edith Rowley, Gladys Birkby, Edna Ackroyd, Harry Bentley, Billy Wright, Betty Rowley, Jim Blackburn.

The Jolly Jesters was a concert party whose members came from St Mark's Church. Their rather formal dress in this photograph belies the down-to-earth family entertainment which delighted audiences in many different venues in the 1950s and 1960s. From left to right: Laurence Harper, Jack Rhodes, Harry Moran, Marion Gribbon *née* Deighton, Mary Saxton, Tony Gribbon, Frank Wilkinson, Harry Firth.

St Mark's Church was opened in 1857 and closed in 2002. It cost £2,500 to build and much of this cost was met by the Earl of Cranbrook, who augmented the endowment given by his late father John Hardy.

Interior of St Mark's Church, 1935. The future use of the building is still to be decided.

This assembled throng were members of St Mark's Church appearing in a production of *The Gondoliers* in 1930.

A Pierrot troop from the 1920s, probably appearing at Hill Top School. From left to right, back row: Albert Thornton, Sidney Tennant, -?-. Middle row: Edith Pickles, Bessie Priestley, Herbert Mounsey, Edith Tordoff, Elsie Tordoff. Front row: Alice Grenhough, Annie Orme.

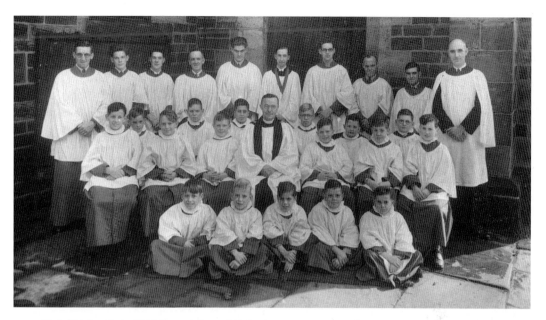

Holy Trinity choir, 1946. From left to right, back row: Hector Smith, Bernard Seed, John Seed, Arthur Rafter, Eric Charlesworth, Harold Wilson (curate), Basil Ackroyd, Bill Hudson, Willie Chapman, Leonard Wilson (organist and choirmaster). Middle row: Vincent Smith, Edward Hill, Bobby Bonner, Eric Smith, Arthur Pratt, Harry Bransby, Revd A.W. Price, Donald Hudson, Alan Bransby, Ewart Pickles, Bernard Ellis, Geoffrey Greenhough, Michael Horsfall. Front row: Frank Howarth, David Wilson, Brian Chapman, Leslie Copley, Peter Lightowlers.

The old Holy Trinity vicarage had the look of the 'sinister dark house' of scary stories. It was demolished in the 1960s and its site and the surrounding fields were swallowed up by the Wesley/Belmont estate.

This old postcard shows a Whitsuntide gathering in Victoria Square, 1921.

A colourfully dressed group of young men from Holy Trinity in the early part of the twentieth century. Second from the left in the middle row is David Wood, who became the Low Moor 'bobby' (see chapter five, 'Everyday People').

The balconies in Holy Trinity were removed in the 1950s and the pulpit relocated, but the church still retains many interesting features, including the many plaques erected to local dignitaries which contain a wealth of historical information.

A rare view of the inside of Holy Trinity, probably taken in the 1950s and looking up the nave from the chancel. A modern meeting room with lift access has been built in recent years at the back of the church and the pews removed from the side aisles.

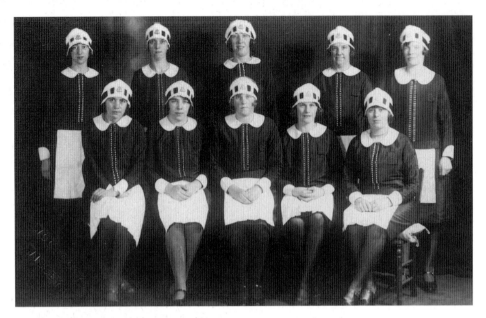

Ladies-in-waiting? Holy Trinity, *c.* 1930. From left to right, back row: Ivy Illingworth, Mrs Proudler, Nellie Hodgson, Eva Rhodes, Mrs Rafter. Front row: Mary Ellen Bramley, Nellie Deighton, Elsie Deighton, Eva Simpson, Ida Tordoff.

Children from Holy Trinity's Central Sunday School (which met at Scott's School), *c.* 1938. They included Mary Dunning and Pat White (third and fourth left, next to back row) and Pat Fallah (fifth left, front row – to the right of the girl in a dark cardigan). In the background are Chapel House Buildings, whilst Upper Park House can be seen across the fields which now accommodate the Wesley/Belmont estate.

Combined service on Wyke recreation ground, *c.* 1953. The singing is conducted by Mr Herman Greenhough of the Temperance Hall, accompanied by the Bradford Salvation Army band.

Young people from St Mary's Church, Wyke pose outside the Exchange Station, Bradford prior to setting off on an excursion to Davos in Switzerland..

In 1844 the Ecclesiastical Commissioners formed the Township of Wyke into a Church District. The parish church of St Mary was built in 1847 with the support of the Low Moor Iron Company and its first vicar, the Revd W. Houlbrook.

St Mary's Church choir and the Revd Denis Wade, *c.* 1960

Above and below: A rare look into the former Zion chapel in Garden Field. After closing in 1926 it was converted into a 'picture house' for silent films with piano accompaniment. Closed down again in 1931 it was then used as a billiard hall. It re-opened as the Hippodrome Cinema in 1937 and after undergoing renovations was renamed the Star Cinema in 1950, with the programme of films changing three times a week. A feature of the 'Star' was the double seats used by courting couples. Following a small fire in 1959 the cinema closed and has since been used as an engineering workshop and a joiners/shopfitters business.

The Salvation Army hut, situated at the top of Mayfield on Huddersfield Road. It was used for services and social events. It was demolished in the 1960s.

Members of the Salvation Army Wyke Corps in front of its headquarters in Huddersfield Road. The 'army' was famous for its brass band and 'Penny Magic Lantern Shows'. With numbers diminishing the corps was finally disbanded in the late 1950s.

After worshipping for many years in Binks Cottages, Wyke Lane, the first Methodist church was erected in Huddersfield Road in 1869 and officially opened in 1871. The Sunday School extension was added in 1913. The church was involved in the life of the community for many years, taking part in united church events and hosting the Wyke horticultural shows. When the building was demolished the foundations were found to have been very shallow indeed. The Sunday School was converted in 1988 into a dual-purpose building used for services and social events.

Wyke Methodist Church Highlights Concert Party, 1941/42. From left to right, back row: Leslie Boland, Bernard Davies, Donald Littlewood, Roy Bennett, Donald Woodcock, Richard Griffiths, Geoffrey Boughton. Front row: Peter Wright, Audrey Littlewood (née Lee), Norman Smith, Annie Freda Smith, Laurie Jones.

Westfield Independent Church, Rose Queen Day, 1947. From left to right, back row: Renee Byford, June Schofield, -?-, -?-, Nancy Briggs, Mollie Emsley, Catherine Young, Eva Broomhead. Front row: Pat Wolsey, Betty Schofield, Doreen Emsley, -?-, -?-, -?-, Angela Young, Molly Hall.

Members of the Westfield Glee Club entertaining residents in an old people's home in Lightcliffe in 1971. The club was formed in 1961 and has presented concerts of choral music, giving pleasure to many in the local community. Some years ago the name was changed to the Westfield Male Voice Choir. From left to right, back row: Wilfred Jones, -?-, Harry Crampton, Tom Ellis, Kenneth Mead, Dorothy Emsley (pianist), -?-, Leslie Crampton, -?-, Eddie Healey, -?-.

Members of the Wyke Temperance Mission were very active producing shows by Gilbert and Sullivan, and in later years pantomimes, and taking part in the Wyke drama festivals. This is the cast of *Mother Goose*, *c.* 1950. From left to right, back row: B. Dalton, S. Pearson, J. Hudson, S. Rishman, J. Smith, B. Gautry, M. Hudson, M. Kellett, J. Gautry, W. Harding, B. Jagger. Middle row: E. Brown, W. Jones, E. Broadbent, P. Jagger, J. Pearson, P. Rushworth, L. Jones, D. Illingworth, M. Foster. Front row: ? Hargreaves, B. Broadbent , P. Broadbent, B. Lee, M. Emmett, -?-, P. Harris, L. Healey, B. Sheard, J. Hargreaves, I. Brown, -?-, R. Garside, -?-, -?-, H. Brown, K. Barker.

Wyke Church Scout troop, *c.* 1916. The scoutmaster was Arthur Hanson.

The Temperance Movement established their first hall in Wyke in 1860, but the original building was demolished and replaced in 1904 by this one in Towngate. The hall was used on many occasions for community events including the Annual Old Folk's Treat – tea and concert – long before the days of Darby and Joan clubs and other modern-day senior citizens groups. Because of the falling number of members and the deterioration of the building the last service was held in 1984.

A Wyke Gospel Hall ladies' outing, during the 1920s. With an open-topped charabanc and puddles in the road, the ladies are hoping for better weather on the journey and at their destination.

The Wyke Gospel Hall girls class, winners of the annual Bradford Covenanters Sports Day held at Northcliffe playing fields, c. 1947. From left to right, back row: Hannah Walker, Sheila Greenough, Doreen Stillings, Doreen Tremlett, Doreen Clough, Bessie Stillings. Middle row: Brenda Hirst, Alice Hirst, Hazel Hirst, Enid Greenough, Margaret Biglands, Doreen Hirst. Two girls in the centre not known. Front row: Maureen Breaks, Anne Chadburn, -?-, Freda Wheeler, Mary Stillings, Marjorie Tremlett, Rita Wilkinson.

Interior of the Gospel Hall, Storr Hill. The building is still there but is now used as business premises.

Lower Wyke is one of four Moravian settlements established in Yorkshire in the middle of the eighteenth century. The original church was built in 1753 and replaced by a larger building in 1775. This shows the church in 1945.

The Ivy House was the Moravian girls boarding school which was behind the church. It is now a private house.

four

Working Days

LOWMOOR

COLD BLAST
PIG IRON

ROBERT HEATH
& LOW MOOR LTD.
LOWMOOR IRONWORKS
BRADFORD,
YORKSHIRE

Left: The front of a six-page leaflet from around 1920, which explained all one needed to know about cold blast pig iron! Robert Heath's were justifiably proud of its world-famous product. The company's 'Better Bed' coal provided an extremely pure coke that did not rely on high temperatures to remove the impurities found in inferior material. At the time, 250 tons of iron were produced at Low Moor each week.

Below: Early 1900s views of Low Moor New Ironworks at the New Biggin, New Works Road. The late Norman Ellis, in his book *Low Moor – the Beginning of a Journey*, told of his memories of the many horses from the Low Moor Company being driven up Park Road on an evening when their work was finished. Here we can see some of the carts they pulled, bearing strong resemblances to the carts used on farms.

LOW MOOR NEW IRON WORKS.

The notice on the gas lamp at the entrance to the New Biggin works warns that there is 'No entry except on business'. The picture shows the winding gear and chimney.

LOW MOOR IRON WORKS

The kilns and the engine house at the ironworks. Coal is being moved around the works on the mineral roads in these conical-shaped wagons.

The hexagonal building stood near the New Works Road (Long Wall Side) entrance to the ironworks and housed the original offices. The postcard carrying this photograph was sent on 30 July 1909 to A. Woodcock Esq. who was staying at 'Southville' on Rutland Street in Filey, at the premises of Mrs F. Simpson. It is signed 'Richd'. Richard Woodcock was a manager at the works and Albert was probably his cousin. It seems to have been typical Bradford summer weather, as it has been raining and hay is spoiling in the fields. Richard mentions that some of their customers are sending out little printed forms advising people that they are taking holidays from 30 July to 9 August. Is this the beginning of Bank Holiday week closures? In Bradford the textile mills would close for Bowling Tide the following week.

Koppers coke ovens, 1913. Dr Heinrich Koppers invented the by-product coke oven with a single or cross regenerator, which became a feature of every modern coke oven system. He incorporated the H. Koppers Company in 1912, which was eventually purchased by American industrialists.

The railway station at Low Moor was closed down in 1965, but there is good news: there is likely to be a new station opening within the next few years.

The railway tracks pass near to the 'Rowdy Dowdy' dam. The house at Woodhouse Hill can be seen on the right. It would be many years hence when the M606 and the Euroway trading estate formed part of the horizon.

The railway lines lead under Cleckheaton Road and into Low Moor station.

Without the caption on the postcard this picture might have seemed mundane but King George V may just have been catching a glimpse of our local area on that summer's day in 1912.

Above and below: There was not much left of the Low Moor gasworks (above) or the railway signal box (below) after the terrible events of 21 August 1916. Thirty-nine people died and many were injured when an explosion at the munitions works off New Works Road spread to the gasworks. Owing to wartime censorship no direct mention was made of the incident in the press. It was the greatest tragedy Low Moor had ever known. A plaque in Oakenshaw Park commemorates the explosion and the statue erected to the memory of the six firemen who died was recently transferred from Scholemoor cemetery to the West Yorkshire Fire Service headquarters at Birkenshaw.

Low Moor Explosion, August 21st, 1916.　　　　ewsbury

The custom of 'Blowing the Horn' existed in Wyke and was only discontinued in the early 1900s. The horn was blown from Manor House on summer mornings at five o'clock, and at six o'clock in the winter, as a summons to the day's work. This interesting relic is still in existence, having passed through the hands of the successive Lords of the Manor until it came into the possession of Mr Harold Stead, a local solicitor. It is now in the hands of his grandson, a Mr Murray, who owns an art gallery in London and resides in Norfolk.

Here the band leads a procession of miners' dependants through the village during the National Miners' Strike of 1912. The banner reads 'Please Help' and they were obviously soliciting donations.

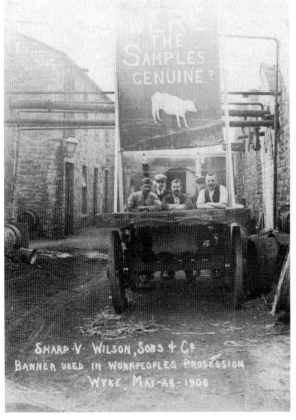

SHARP V. WILSON, SONS & Cᵒ
BANNER USED IN WORKPEOPLES PROCESSION
WYKE. MAY-28-1908

Above and left: These two photographs depict the workpeople's demonstration of 28 May 1908 against the closure of Pickle Bridge dyeworks, at that time owned by Wilson & Sons, successors to Sharp & Binns. The closure, which threw 200 Wyke people out of work, resulted from the finding of a dead heifer near the dyeworks' culvert. The heifer was presumed to have been poisoned by contaminated water and James Sharp, who owned the land, initiated court proceedings against Wilson's. The Bradford city analyst gave evidence about samples that had allegedly been taken from the animal's stomach which seemed to suggest it had been poisoned. Wilson's employees, however, couldn't accept the analyst's findings as genuine and stated that they used the same beck water every day for making tea without any ill effects. The protest march paraded from Clare Road to New Road Side and ended with a meeting of between 4-5,000 people in a field at the top of Wilson Road. The banners read 'LIVE AND LET LIVE' and 'WERE THE SAMPLES GENUINE?'. The protracted litigation ultimately resulted in Wilson & Sons going into voluntary liquidation in 1911.

John Hinds' mill – another textile mill in the district – situated at the corner of High Fernley Road and Woodside Road. It was demolished in the 1970s and replaced by High Fernley School.

In addition to coal mining and textiles and chemical manufacturing, farming (mainly dairy farming) was an important employer for the residents of Wyke. In 1847 there were about twenty-three farms, reduced to fifteen by 1940. In 1972 only five were left, two of which kept pigs as well as dairy herds. This shows Brick House Farm, which stood on Green Lane.

Above: The tram terminus outside Wyke Board School. The back of the postcard shows it was produced for 'T. Turner, Post Office, Wyke'.

Right: The list of destinations taken from a local tram. The driver would turn a handle which transferred the long strip from one roller to another, and the intended destination was thus displayed at the front of the vehicle.

PARK AVENUE
WYKE
BAILIFF BRIDGE
BANKFOOT
ODSAL
LOW MOOR
BOWLING OLD LANE
THORNBURY
LITTLE HORTON
WIBSEY
SOUTHFIELD LANE
WHITE HORSE
GREAT HORTON
HORTON BANK TOP
QUEENSBURY

Birkby's brickworks. This photograph was taken from the Wilson Road side of the works and shows some of the ovens. The works, which were started by Henry Birkby in 1869, continued until the 1970s. Many houses in the area were built with Birkby's bricks. In 1899 Mr Birkby was returned as councillor for the Wyke ward and served on the Council for three years.

Birkby's brickworks' system of transport. The movement of bricks is heavy work and this small rail system was used at the rear of the works to transport materials and bricks to different internal sites.

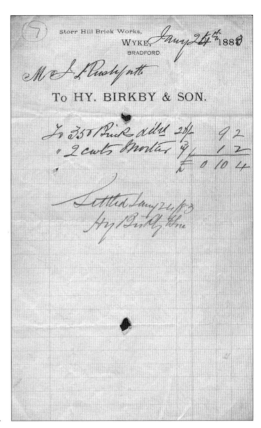

Storr Hill Brick Works,
WYKE,
BRADFORD.

Jany 24th 1888

M J L Rushforth

To HY. BIRKBY & SON.

Right: How much would it cost to build a house in 1883? Here we have a bill issued by Birkby's brickworks to Mr Rushforth for 10/4d which covered the delivery of both bricks and mortar – and was settled immediately!

Below: The Wyke viaduct (270 yards long) was built in 1873 by the Lancashire & Yorkshire and Great Central Railways in order to link Bradford to the London line. The branch line left the main line at Wyke Junction and swept round to the Wyke viaduct which straddled the Leeds and Whitehall Road. Passenger traffic was carried until 1948 when subsidence limited its use to goods trains, which ran until 1952 when the line was closed. Part of the viaduct was demolished in 1986.

A.H. Marks Chemicals, photographed before the Second World War. The firm was ounded in 1881 by the family of Samson Breaks who, in 1913, sold his house and business to Augustus H. Marks. Between 1898 and 1917 the firm began to manufacture picric acid, having obtained orders from the government even so far back as the Boer War. In 1917, following the Wyke Lane explosion, the Breaks family severed all connections with the firm. The business is now known as A.H. Marks & Co. Ltd and has become the UK's largest privately owned and independent chemical manufacturing company.

The Pepper Lee Mill complex covered several textile mills. This included Pepper Lee, Goodman Abbott & Wright, Benson Turners, and Barracloughs. The mills were situated in the hollow at the side of the Huddersfield Road and close to Station Road, Wyke. Sadly, with the demise of the textile industry, these mills ceased trading in the early 1980s.

Above and below: Goodman, Abbott & Wright was one of the local textile mills which could rely on the local population to keep trade going. Here, probably, in the 1950s, we glimpse the inside of the 'Warping and Winding' department and meet some of the workers.

Pickle Bridge dyeworks, Wyke, was started in these premises in 1862 by James Sharp, very close to the site of the railway line. In 1899 he sold out to his brother John. The dyeworks continued to manufacture until the early 1900s.

Wyke station. An impressive-looking gentleman (on the right) awaits the train which will take him to his place of business. On the other platform railway workers await arrivals. The bridge spanning the lines allows access along Station Road to Norwood Green.

five

Everyday People

Above left: Standing in the back garden of No. 5 Sugden Street, Wyke Bottoms, are brothers George and Harry Barraclough (centre and sitting), *c.* 1904. On the right is Herman Mitchell who married their sister, Alice. The identity of the man on the left is unknown.

Above right: This time at the front door of No. 5, George and his younger brother Harry stand with their mother Sarah Ellen Barraclough (*née* Brown), *c.* 1907. Even the cat gets in the picture!

Left: Barraclough was a popular name in the area. This is Dan Barraclough, his wife Sarah and children Martha and Tom, *c.* 1900. Dan's farm was compulsory purchased to make way for North Bierley cemetery and he has the distinction of being buried on what was his own land!

Left: The Sykes brothers of Low Moor. From left to right: Joshua Pyrah Sykes, Harold Pyrah and Alfred Pyrah Sykes in the early 1900s.

Below: This is the Low Moor wedding of Reginald Bolton and Hilda Pyrah. From left to right, standing: Samuel Bolton, Eddie Simpson, Reginald, Hilda, Emily Booth. Seated: Ann Bolton, Elizabeth Pyrah in the early 1900s.

Above left: Sergeant Francis Lewis Wood (born 1860), the first of the two 'Bobby' Woods, who served in Low Moor. Pictured with him is his son Cecil and daughter Kathleen.

Above right: Sergeant David Lewis Wood (born 1892), Francis' other son.

Their quiffs place them firmly in the middle of the 1950s. From left to right: Paul Guy, Jack Brear, Tony Ackroyd.

A gathering of neighbours and friends from New Works Road to celebrate the eightieth birthday of Constance Dobson in 1936. From left to right, back row: Mary Elizabeth Dobson, Mr and Mrs Ormonroyd, -?-, Mary Hannah Holroyd, Tom Hoyle, -?-. Middle row: Stanley Dobson, Harry Hoyle, -?-, Edith Whaley, Mrs Stobart (mother of Jack), -?-, -?-. Front row: Jack Stobart, Mrs Stobart, Geoffrey Dobson Constance Dobson, Kenneth Dobson, Susan Law.

The men have not been able to be identified but the background reveals the site as the spare land that stood between Huddersfield Road and Oxley Street.

Right: Ten years on from the end of the First World War, the cenotaph is unveiled at the bottom of Netherlands Avenue. Winter appeared to have started early that year – a grim reminder of the hardships suffered by those who fought and died for their country. In only a few short years the names of more Low Moor men would form a new list.

Below: The front page of the Unveiling Ceremony programme. The memorial was erected by public subscription and the officials on the committee were J.T. Cliffe (chairman), E. Holroyd (vice-chairman), F. Booth (treasurer) and H. Holroyd (honorary secretary). The cost of erection was just over £400, the money being raised by donations and proceeds from local concerts.

Below right: Inside the programme.

LOW MOOR CENOTAPH,
NETHERLANDS AVENUE,

Unveiling and Dedication

of the War Memorial

To the Men who gave their lives
in the European War,
1914–1918.

"Their Names Liveth for Evermore."

The Ceremony will take place at 3 p.m.

On Saturday, November 10th, 1928.

J. T. CLIFFE, Esq. will preside.

The Unveiling will be performed by
THE LORD MAYOR (Ald. H. Thornton Pullan).

TO the Sacred Memory of the Men of Low Moor, who served their King and Country, and lost their lives in the European War,

1914–1918.

This is a Memorial of our Gratitude and to their Honour.

This Memorial was erected by Public Subscription, and was
Unveiled November 10th, 1928.

Willie Barraclough.
Sargent Bentley.
Herbert V. Blower.
Arthur Borrow.
John A. Bower.
Fred Boyes.
Edward Brayshaw.
Walter Brook.
Thomas Clarkson.
Arthur Coates.
Albert E. Coomber.
William Cordingley.
Harry Dalby.
Albert Downes.
Edward J. Dyson.
Harold Ellis.
Fred Emmett.
Joel Firth.
Peter Firth.
Charles H. Graves.
Norman Hanson.
Sam Hanson.
Cecil Herringshaw.
Harry Holdsworth.
Willie Howard.
Harold Jowett.
Arthur Kellett.
Harry Kershaw.
Fred Lister.
Richard Merrin.
Harold Milnes.
Alfred Parrish.
Albert Pearson.
Leonard Pollard.
Willie Potts.
Richard H. Priestley.
Willie Priestley.
John Rhodes.
Wilson Riley.
Houghton E. Sargent.
Albert Schofield.
Walter Stainthorpe.
Joseph Stead.
Ralph Stobart.
Percy Sutcliffe.
Harry Sykes.
Willie Tordoff.
Fred Wainwright.
Tom Wakefield.
Arthur Wells.
John J. Whitaker.
Albert Wilson.
John W. Wood.
Albert Woodcock.
Leslie A. Woodcock.
Harry T. Woodhead.
Willie Woodhead.
Francis J. Woodhouse.

"They shall grow not old.
As we that are left grow old;
Age shall not weary them,
Nor the years condemn:
At the going down of the sun,
And in the morning,
We will remember them."
Laurence Binyon.

Above left: George Alfred Stockley, whose family were one of the first to move into Griffe Road on the newly built Shirley Manor estate in 1932. Not everyone had the luxury of an alarm clock and with his long pole George Alfred was the local 'knocker up'.

Above right: His son George Stockley, a boiler-firer at the RNO (known locally as Renovating Yorkshire's Own) works. He later became the projectionist at the Wyke 'Star' Picture House.

Outside the Red Lion public house in 1916 some customers gather with (on the steps) the licensees James and Ann Ellen Keighley.

Above: Ex-servicemen march in Wyke recreation ground in the 1930s, headed by the Low Moor and Wyke British Legion. The Parade Marshall was Wilf Reid, the Standard Escorts Dan P. Ward and Edgar Lumb. Local Brownies take part in the salute.

Left: Is this before lighting in houses was the norm? The lamp oil man takes his huge can around the village and sells to those who depend on oil for lighting.

six

Everyday Places

This viewpoint is above the small wood next to Royds Hall dam. The terraced houses on the middle left are in Common Road. Park Road runs up to their right with a gap where later houses would be built. The hump at the top of the picture was the 'Red Hills', the shale depository and quarry on which the St Abbs estate was built in the 1960s. The large building in the centre was the School Street Primitive Methodist chapel in the early 1900s.

Looking from the top of Delph Hill down to St Mark's Vicarage and across the wood yard to Mather's buildings and the end of Common Road. The cinema is yet to be built. The track of the telegraph poles show where Huddersfield Road winds its way to Odsal Top. On the left horizon is Robertshaw's Mill at Odsal in the early 1900s.

The houses are still there in Park Road but Delf Hill Middle School is no more in the 1970s.

These houses are long gone, but Lower School Street lives on as one of the few streets which are still traceable following the widescale demolition of the Hill Top area in the 1970s.

A view of Fountain Street in the 1960s looking from North Street. The cellar dwellings are under the houses on the middle left.

Fountain Street. The house facing us at the end of the street is still there in Union Road. Note the toilet block halfway down the street. The small shop at the corner was occupied in its latter days by Mr John Hirst in the 1960s.

Fountain Street cellar dwellings in the 1970s.

Many people will remember North Street fisheries, second up on the left. The houses facing down were in Manor Row. This part of Victoria Mills was occupied by Fearnley Rhodes, a spinning company in the 1960s.

Above: The vegetation sprouting from every nook and cranny was an indication that the Council's 1970s clearance programme was about to take effect in Victoria Street.

Left: The large 'R' hanging from the New Inn in Union Street was the sign of the Halifax-based Ramsden's Brewery. The enclosed high-level walkway connected the two parts of Victoria Mills. Mill Street lies beyond them in the 1960s.

Above: The narrow Yorkshire 'setts' and cracked flagstones paved Manor Row as it ran between Union Road and Mill Street. The houses behind the low cottages are still there today but the rest have all gone. The large house in the centre was at the top of North Street and the 'lean-to' roofs on the right are the back of Portland Street in the 1960s.

Left: Mill Street, Low Moor, as it was in March 1966, somewhat muddy at the bottom. The shop just on the bottom left was Gilron's greengrocers. Just off the picture to the right was the Economic Stores, a branch of the Halifax-based grocery chain.

The sun is shining down on School Street in the 1960s. The former Working Men's Club is on the left and the former Primitive Methodist chapel stands opposite, just out of sight.

School Street in the early part of the twentieth century. The Lion Stores was part of the Cleckheaton-based Hillards group. Wilson Street, on the left, had a regularly used slaughterhouse, which kept inquisitive children entertained.

School Street, Low Moor, 1966. What - no cars? Such a narrow main street would be chaos today.

Victoria Square, Low Moor, 1966. That bus shelter was a drafty place to stand in winter! The houses on the left are the back of Wood Row. Albert Hanson's grocers' in the middle latterly went to the dogs – or more accurately the horses – as it became a branch of Ladbrokes! The newsagent's shop on the right was remembered in particular for a previous occupier, Josiah Gill, who also had a small printing works Huddersfield Road.

Left: This well-preserved paper bag is all that is contained in the Low Moor group's archives as a memento of a very popular shop frequented by local ladies.

Below: The remains of Willy Slater's cottage on Old Hill Top. Willy did carrier work and kept his horse in the adjoining cottage in the 1970s!

If you stand on this part of Hird Road/Worsnop Street today you might see members of the catering staff taking a well-earned breather at the back door of the Guide Post Hotel. The houses facing us were named East View in the 1960s.

Slicer Buildings were named after the Slicer family who lived here for over fifty years. They were situated next to the British Queen pub, the gable of which can just be seen on the right. Edwin Slicer was a watchmaker, and a clock was mounted on the corner of the right-hand outside wall. The motorcycle shop had previously been a dress shop, a café and Bob Slicer's DIY shop in the 1960s.

The sign for the British Queen public house is the only remaining landmark of this scene in Huddersfield Road. Slicer Buildings are on the left. The bottom of Common Road is in the far distance, and the sign of the Victoria inn (also known as 'The Drop') can be seen above the parked car. The fish and chip shop and the Lion Stores were at the end of School Street. The newsagents (formerly Eastwood's then Shaw's) stood next to the residence of Mr George Booth, the neighbourhood undertaker.

A point of reference between the old and the new: the shops in Victoria Square waiting for its demolition, whilst the new co-op is being erected in Huddersfield Road.

Odsal House was situated in the small woodland off Huddersfield Road, behind where Sedbergh Boys' Club now stands. It was built for Charles Hardy, a founder member of the Low Moor Company. During its later life it was used as a school for the blind and also for the deaf. It was demolished in the 1960s.

Ivy Terrace (now known as Hird Road) contains some of the oldest houses in Low Moor.

The Harold Club may still look very similar today as it did in the early part of the twentieth century but the trams are long gone, as are the 'fishbone' topped telegraph poles and the smoky chimneys of the ironworks.

This drinking fountain, removed from the top of New Works Road around the time of the Second World War, had a lower area for dogs, and an upper one for their owners and passers-by.

Morley Carr is the area adjacent to New Works Road, below Carr Lane. There were only two principal streets – King Street and George Street. Industrial units and warehousing replaced them in the 1970s.

Holly Hall, on the border of the Low Moor-Wyke boundary. Mr and Mrs W. Barraclough lived here between 1930and 1950. Three cottages were attached to the hall and were occupied by people who helped in various duties within the house. Mr Barraclough was a florist and sold flowers from the stable or barn. He was also an antique collector and an entomologist and had a valuable collection of butterflies. Mr and Mrs Barraclough are both buried in St Mark's Church graveyard, Low Moor.

The architect, contractor and workmen pose during the building of the Victoria Hall in Storr Hill in 1897. The building later housed Wyke library and swimming pool and is still in use as a warehouse and workshop. The man with the trowel, in the foreground, is Harry Holdsworth.

The Yeoman's House (or Manor or Farm) in Towngate is dated 1675 and has often been thought of as a manor house, but there is no proof of this because the deeds were lost many years ago. Structurally it is very similar to other manor houses in the area. Is it a coincidence that it is almost equidistant from Lower Wyke and Norwood Green Manor houses? Used in the twentieth century as a farm, a builder's yard, a shop and a café, at the time of publication it is occupied by a charity shop.

Towngate, Wyke – with the leading shops including the post office. Further up the road is the Oddfellows Arms public house, now simply called the Oddfellows and known to many as the 'Top Odd'. This is because lower down the road is the Oddfellows Hall, another public house. The road has altered very little since the Edwardian era apart from cosmetic changes.

The view looking the other way in Towngate in 1932.

The cottages which face the main post office and block of shops in Towngate have now all been converted to business premises. Here, in 1922, the group of men in the distance appear to be gathering for a march or some other kind of demonstration.

Towngate in the 1960s. Little has changed except for the absence of the butcher's shop behind the car on the left of the picture. This shop has now been demolished leaving an open space.

The Lion Stores traded in Towngate for several decades until the late 1960s, early 1970s. The building was eventually demolished but the cottage property beyond the shop is still occupied and used as a solicitor's office, opticians and shoe repairers. The premises on the left-hand side of the photograph was called Prowses Tinners and is now a fish and chip shop.

Ramsden's Butchers, originally started by Sam Ramsden in the early part of the twentieth century. Sam's son Harry (in photograph) joined his father in the shop as he grew up and continued selling high-quality meats until his retirement in the late 1970s.

Greenwood's tailors, Towngate, Wyke. You didn't have to go to town to get a well-tailored suit; the local tailor could make something just as smart and often not as expensive. Many people would be able to buy a suit length at a reasonable price and then take it to Mr Greenwood. How smart they would look!

Carr Road, Wyke, a very old street which ran from Towngate into Huddersfield Road. On the right-hand side of the picture, in the low property, there has been a fish and chips business for many years. The street was known to many local people as 'Well Lane'. It is thought that one of the many wells in the district was situated in this area. Since the building of old people's flats, part of this road has been used and is no longer a through road.

The Cooperative Buildings, Huddersfield Road/Carr Road, were part of the Brighouse Cooperative Stores. In the buildings shown, there were departments covering butchery, greengrocery, grocery, drapery, shoes and, in the 1940s and '50s, a pharmacy shop. Butter was weighed out from a large block, treacle was poured into a jar and loose flour was weighed on demand – mostly in stones, or half-stones. Each customer who became a member was given a registered number and dividends were paid to customers half yearly. It is amazing how many people today can still immediately recite their own, or even their mother's, 'divvy' number.

The Halfway House Inn is situated on the main Bradford to Huddersfield road. The covered wagon is probably bringing a delivery. Note the long clothing, white aprons and bowler hat – so popular at one time. The stables were at the rear of the building.

The photographer has obviously attracted the curiosity of the mothers and children in Clare Road. The girls in the centre in the white aprons are Nellie and Winfred Smith (who became Mrs Hirst). Little did they realize that a hundred or so years later they would be 'stars' of a local history book!

The local street trader – with his own transport and horses in tandem – poses in Clare Road in the 1920s. The exterior of the houses have changed very little in the last eighty years.

Above: Houses in Temperance Field, Wyke. Originally called Teetotal Field, it was possibly changed when Wyke Township was incorporated into North Bierley Urban District Council. The house numbers are not consecutive and must be a postman's nightmare!

Left: The Wyke Guide Post or Mile Stone was situated at the corner of the green where Wyke Lane joined Towngate until around 1957 when the area was purchased by the Bradford Corporation. It was then taken to Bolling Hall for safekeeping. It was erected in 1733 and bears the names of William Richardson and John Hanson, as well as the mileage to Leeds, Bradford and Halifax – originally spelt Leedes, Bradford and Hallifacx. Under the 1555 Highways Act, all the inhabitants of the village above the position of hired labourer had to meet once a year with horses and carts to give six days' labour in repairing the roads. They appointed overseers from their own number to ensure that the work was done satisfactorily. Gradually, after the 1706 Turnpike Trust Act was passed, the practice was discontinued. The Guide Post was removed from Bolling Hall in 2001 at the instigation of Wyke Local History Group and is now situated to the rear of St Mary's Church.

Above: This aerial photograph shows Wyke before the construction of the library at the junction of Woodside Road and Huddersfield Road. The bungalows at the top of Wilson Road were yet to be built and part of Wyke Crescent stands in isolation at the bottom right of the photograph.

Opposite above: Sparrow Park at the bottom of Green Lane, Wyke. It was a small, enclosed, piece of land which is reputed to have been used as a meeting place of local Luddites.

Opposite below: Blankney Grange, Lower Wyke. A very ornate and gabled building built in the 1860s by Dr Witteron MD who had a surgery in Carr Lane, Low Moor. In 1922 it was occupied by Mr Arthur Davy. In 1947 it was converted into an old people's home with additional sleeping accommodation being added to the building. After being closed in the early 1990s, it was sold to a private company and reopened, after renovation, as a psychiatric hospital.

Shirley Manor, Wyke – a many gabled building set in large grounds. This was the home of the Sharp family, owners of the Pickle Bridge dyeworks and reputed to be named after the Charlotte Brontë novel *Shirley*. A tunnel was put under the turnpike road for the use of Mr Sharp to enable him to reach the works without crossing the main road. After being used for some years as a residence for the elderly, it was closed and later demolished after being damaged by fire.

Achnacarry, Griffe Road, Wyke. This was the home of Mr and Mrs Cameron and their family, Marion, Alec, Emma and Catherine. Catherine was, for a number of years, in practice as a doctor in Wyke. A wooden seat has been placed in her memory outside the main door of Westfield United Reform Church.

Carr Hall (or Carr Head). This was the home of William Wainman, one of the largest landowners at the time of the Enclosure Acts. It was a plain square building with an ornamental balustrade as its only decoration. During the Second World War the Hall was used by the Fire Service and was eventually demolished. Wainman Street is named after William.

Cow Close Cottages, Wyke, built down Knowle Lane, in the seventeenth century. The photograph shows part of the farm complex. The farm has mullioned windows and also a triangular slab above the doorway. It is built in gritstone with lighter pointing. Because of the proximity to the roads which have resulted since the M62 was built, some of the land belonging to the farm has been taken for the access roads to Bradford.

High Fernley Hall and Farm, photographed in 1996. Built in1678 by the Richardson family of Bierley Hall, and situated between Wyke and Horse Close Bridge in Judy Woods, it has a beautiful view over the surrounding countryside. What is now the mistal used to be the house and over the door is a diamond-shaped sign with the letters 'WM', the initials of William and Mary Richardson.

Horse Close Cottages are situated in the fields between Royds Hall and Judy Woods. Each cottage had its own garden with creepers adorning the walls. The local poet Charlotte Oates who lived here in the late 1800s gave them the name Daisy Cottages. In the 1930s, '40s and '50s, Mr Harry Dalby was the Wood Ranger and lived with his family in one of these cottages.

Woodside Farm, down High Fernley Road, was originally erected as a wooden building. In its present form it dates from around 1503.

The old Manor House in Lower Wyke, occupied at one time by James Barraclough, Steward of the Low Moor Company. It was built at three different periods: the oldest portion of the building is at the back, the centre portion was built in 1614, and the front, facing Wyke (Wike) Lane, was built at a later period. It was built by the Empsall family, and on the doorway, at the back of the house, is their coat of arms, the Rose of England, and the date 1694.

Other local titles published by Tempus

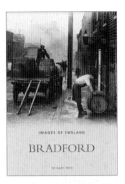

Bradford

DR GARY FIRTH

This selection of more than 200 old photographs recalls Bradford during the period of over half a century from 1880 to the 1950s. The images recall buildings and streets long gone, while stirring memories of the way of life of men, women and children going about their work and play in this busy, vibrant, manufacturing city.

0 7524 3019 X

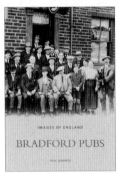

Bradford Pubs

PAUL JENNINGS

This fascinating volume tells the story of Bradford's pubs over two centuries. Illustrated with over 150 old photographs, plans and advertisements, the collection recalls the pubs, the people who ran them, the customers who frequented them, and the brewers who supplied and usually owned them. The reader will glimpse the pub in all its many guises, from the coaching inns of the early nineteenth century, to the splendid Victorian gin palaces and humble backstreet beer houses, through to the modern pubs of the twenty-first century.

0 7524 3302 4

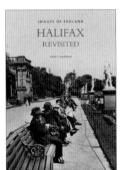

Halifax Revisited

VERA CHAPMAN

Halifax is characterised by steep slopes and deep valleys, sett-paved streets and nearby moorland. It has an industrial past of woollen mills, canals and railways, the wharves and stations of which liberally dot the countryside. The town today reflects the changes wrought by the Victorians who created broad streets and fine buildings. This collection of over 200 archive images illustrates the history of Halifax as it once was and records how the town has developed since the mid-eighteenth century.

0 7524 3047 5

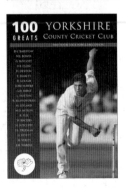

Yorkshire County Cricket Club: 100 Greats

MICK POPE AND PAUL DYSON

This book features 100 of the cricketers who have shaped Yorkshire CCC; from George Anderson, who first played for Yorkshire in 1850 – before the official club was constituted – to Matthew Hoggard, who received the coveted county cap in 2000. This book gives a glimpse of the characters, often colourful, sometimes controversial and invariably commanding – portrayed through short biographies, accompanied by a photograph and statistical profile.

0 7524 2179 4

If you are interested in purchasing other books published by Tempus, or in case you have difficulty finding any Tempus books in your local bookshop, you can also place orders directly through our website

www.tempus-publishing.com